SWEDEN

Bo Kage Carlson

MACDONALD YOUNG BOOKS

First published in 1999 by Macdonald Young Books
An imprint of Wayland Publishers Ltd
© Macdonald Young Books 1999

Macdonald Young Books
61 Western Road
Hove
East Sussex
BN3 1JD

Find Macdonald Young Books on the Internet at
http://www.myb.co.uk

Design and typesetting Roger Kohn Designs
Commissioning editor Rosie Nixon
Editor Merle Thompson
Picture research Shelley Noronha
Maps János Márffy

We are grateful to the following for permission
to reproduce photographs:
Front cover: Robert Harding, *above* (K Hart);
Britstock, *below* (Hans Stroud);
B & C Alexander, pages 9, 12 *below right,* 14, 14/15, 19,
38, 42; Britstock, page 10 *below left* (Hans Strand); Bruce
Coleman, pages 13 (J Jurka), 15 (J Jurka), 32 (J Jurica);
C M Dixon, page 8 *above centre*; Genesis, page 43; Leslie
Garland, pages 11 *bottom right*, 16, 28/29 *below right*, 36
below left; Robert Harding, pages 7 (M Jenner), 29 *above
right* (C Andreason), 31 (C Andreason), 37; Papillo, pages
10/11 *above centre*, 22 *below right*; Pica Press, pages 18
(B Larsson-Ask), 22 *above left* (B Larsson-Ask), 23
(A Wiklund), 24 (J Henriksson), 25 (J Henriksson), 26 (P Ulf),
27 *above left* (P Ydreskog), 27 *below right* (J Holzer), 28
above left (P Flato), 30 (M Lundberg), 33 (L R Jansson), 34
(C Jonson), 35 (T Sica), 36 *above right* (G Ludmark), 39;
40/41; Tony Stone, 8 *below centre* (L Gullachsen), 12 *above
left* (C Ehlers), 20 (T Wood); WPL, page 21.

The statistics given in this book are the most up to date
available at the time of going to press

Printed in Hong Kong by Wing King Tong

A CIP catalogue record for this book is available from
the British Library

ISBN: 0 7500 2617 0

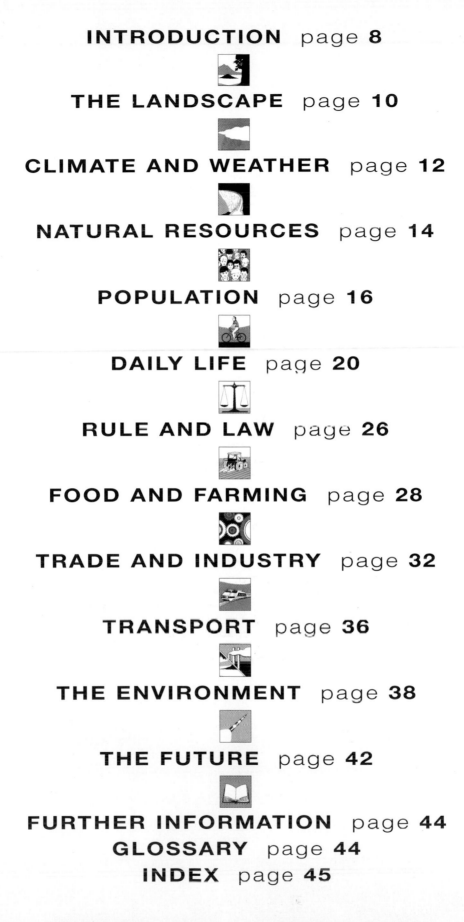

CONTENTS

Words that are explained in the glossary are printed in
SMALL CAPITALS the first time they are mentioned in the text.

✚ INTRODUCTION

Modern Sweden is a highly industrialized country and its people enjoy an excellent standard of living. This, however, is a recent development, that did not begin until the end of the 19th century.

The country was first settled some 13,000 years ago, when the last ICE AGE was coming to an end. First to arrive were reindeer hunters, who came from the European continent across a land bridge connecting Denmark with Sweden. They were followed by fishermen, herdsmen and, eventually, by farmers. They gradually spread through the full length of the country, but even today Sweden is thinly populated. This is especially true of the northern part of the country, where the climate is severe.

The first Swedes lived in small communities, but gradually a number of kingdoms were formed. Most people made a poor living from the land. From the 9th to the 12th centuries, some, known as Vikings, left their homes for long periods travelling by ship to trade, to plunder or to find new land. Many found their way to England and France, while others sailed down the Russian rivers as far as Turkey and Greece.

In about AD 1000, the smaller kingdoms were united into one country. Stockholm became its capital from about 1250.

▼ *Riddarholmen (Knights' Island) in central Stockholm with the old town and the Royal Castle in the background.*

◄ *A memorial stone at Alskog on the island of Gotland showing the eight-legged horse of the Viking god Odin.*

Swedish kings also ruled over Finland for hundreds of years and, for a briefer period, over Norway. Since 1905, however, Sweden has not had any overseas colonies or departments. There are, however, millions of people of Swedish origin living abroad. This is because, from about 1850–1950, approximately 1.5 million people emigrated to other countries, especially to America, to escape poverty.

As industrialization arrived late in Sweden, in 1900, 75% of people still lived in the countryside. During the 20th century, Sweden has rapidly changed into an industrial country with over 80% of its inhabitants living in urban areas. Today, Sweden is best known for its Volvo cars and Ericsson telephone systems.

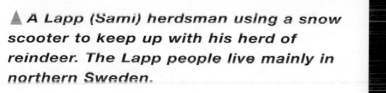

▲ *A Lapp (Sami) herdsman using a snow scooter to keep up with his herd of reindeer. The Lapp people live mainly in northern Sweden.*

SWEDEN AT A GLANCE

● Area: 449,964 square kilometres, of which 39,000 square kilometres or 9% consists of inland waters
● Population: (1997) 8.9 million
● Population density: 19.8 per square kilometre
● Capital: Stockholm, population (1997) 727,000 (Greater Stockholm has a population of 1.75 million)
● Other main cities (1997): Göteborg 457,000, Malmö 251,000, Uppsala 186,000
● Highest mountain: Kebnekaise, 2,111 metres
● Largest lake: Vänern, 5,650 square kilometres
● Longest river: Torne älv, 510 kilometres
● Language: Swedish
● Major religion: Christianity (87% of Swedes are members of the Lutheran church)
● Life expectancy: 79 years (81 years for women and 76 years for men)
● Currency: Swedish crowns (kronor), written as SEK. The krona is divided into 100 öre
● Economy: Highly industrialized. Less than 3% of the work force is employed in agriculture and fishing
● Major resources: Iron ore, timber, hydro-electricity, nuclear power
● Major products: Cars and other engineering products, electronic equipment, paper and pulp
● Environmental problems: Air pollution in the larger cities; water pollution from shipping, industry and agriculture

THE LANDSCAPE

Sweden is one of the largest countries in Europe covering about two-thirds of the Scandinavian peninsula. It is long and narrow, stretching almost 1,600 kilometres from north to south, but only 500 kilometres from east to west. Its land border with Norway to the west is 1,600 kilometres long, while the border with Finland to the east stretches for 560 kilometres. A narrow strait, Öresund, less than 4 kilometres wide, separates it from Denmark to the south-west.

The coast line is 2,180 kilometres long and there are several groups of islands or archipelagos. The largest group lies to the east of Stockholm. There are also larger islands, like Gotland and Öland in the Baltic Sea.

A long mountain range runs along the border with Norway. Some peaks reach a height of 2,000 metres. These were once much higher, but they were eroded away during the ice age by the rock and boulders carried in the ice. As the ice

◀ **More than half of Sweden is covered by forests and thousands of lakes dot the landscape. In the north, there are many mountains that have rounded summits.**

◀ A village in a clearing in the forest, overlooking a fertile plain, a landscape that is typically Swedish.

melted, sediments were deposited in the lowland areas, turning them into fertile plains.

To the south and along the coast, there are large lowland plains separated by somewhat higher forest areas, the South Swedish Highlands. About 55% of Sweden is covered by forest, making it one of the most densely forested countries in Europe.

Several large rivers run from the mountains along the borders towards the Baltic Sea. There are also a number of rivers carrying water from the southern highlands. Most rivers have been dammed to provide hydro-electricity, but a few have been preserved for environmental reasons. The Swedish landscape is dotted with lakes. Most of these are small but 4,000 of them cover areas larger than a square kilometre. Some are very large, especially Lake Vänern, the third largest lake of Europe after Lake Ladoga and Lake Onega in Russia.

▼ A view from the mountain top of Sulitelma overlooking Padjelanta National Park, the largest of Sweden's 24 national parks.

KEY FACTS

● The largest lakes are Vänern, 5,648 square kilometres, Vättern, 1,912 square kilometres, Mälaren, 1,140 square kilometres and Hjälmaren, 478 square kilometres.
● Several of the lakes are very deep. Hornavan is 221 metres, Torneträsk 168 metres, Siljan 134 metres and Vättern 128 metres deep.
● Together Klarälven, Lake Vänern and Göta älv form a natural waterway 650 kilometres long, 160 kilometres of which run through Norway.
● Some of Sweden's mountain peaks may well have been as high as those in the Himalayas before they were eroded away.

CLIMATE AND WEATHER

Sweden lies as far north as Siberia and Alaska, areas with an Arctic or near-Arctic climate, and as far south as Denmark, therefore, the climate in southern Sweden is very different from that of the north. For example, it is warm enough for people in the south of the country to begin going to the beach in late May or early June. In the mountains of north-west Lapland, however, people would still be using their skis and skates.

Summers north of the Arctic Circle are short, but the hours of daylight are very long. At the height of summer, the midnight sun does not dip below the horizon.

In the winter, however, the days are very short. In the extreme north, for about two weeks around Christmas, the sun never reaches above the horizon. The variations in daylight between summer and winter are much less notable in southern Sweden. Winters in the north are much colder than in the south. In the extreme north, the average January temperature is 10–15°C below that of the south. In July the difference is only 2–3°C.

The long winters in

▲ *Picnickers in Stockholm, on a pleasant summer day, are watching a yacht race taking place on Riddarfjärden. The City Hall can be seen on the right in the background.*

▲ *The arrival of spring is celebrated all over the country on Walpurgis Night, in April, when bonfires are lit.*

KEY FACTS

● During the winter, the whole of the country is covered with snow. In the northern mountains, the snow is 1,000–2,000 mm deep and lasts for seven to eight months. The south of the country has a blanket of snow, 200–400 mm deep, that lasts for less than two months.

● The highest temperature ever recorded in Sweden is 38°C. The lowest ever, -53°C, was reported in December 1941, from Malgovik, in Lapland.

● Stockholm is on approximately the same latitude as Churchill, Manitoba, in Canada.

northern Sweden mean that the growing season is very short. In some parts of Lapland, there are only 100 days a year when the temperature is high enough for plants to grow. This makes farming difficult. In the southern third of the country, however, plants can grow for about 200 days each year.

However, because of the Gulf Stream, which brings warm water and mild winds from the West Indies across the Atlantic, most of Sweden has a mild maritime climate. In Stockholm, located 60° north of the Equator, the January average is -2.5°C, whereas the world average on that latitude is -15°C.

As the wind blows mainly from the west, the west coast gets more rain than other parts of the country. In some areas, this is as much as 1,000–1,200 mm a year. The eastern coastal areas receive only 600–700 mm. Some inland areas in the north receive even less, because the clouds from the west have deposited their rain over the mountains along the border with Norway.

◀ *In Jukkasjärvi, in Lapland, locals as well as tourists have to travel about on snow scooters.*

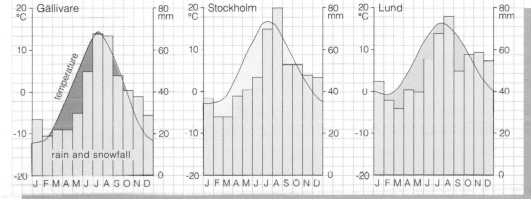

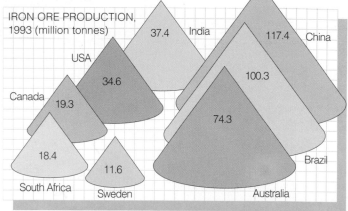

◄ *Iron ore is found underground in Sweden. Most of the deposits are in Lapland.*

IRON ORE PRODUCTION, 1993 (million tonnes)

- USA — 34.6
- India — 37.4
- China — 117.4
- Canada — 19.3
- Brazil — 100.3
- South Africa — 18.4
- Sweden — 11.6
- Australia — 74.3

Iron, wood and water have, for centuries, been key elements in the development of Sweden and are still important for the modern Swedish economy. At first, iron ore was collected in swamps and lakes, but, in the 12th century, production began to increase when the first iron ore mine was opened on the island of Utö, in the Baltic Sea. In the 19th century, the export of wood helped to finance the development of industries and railways in Sweden. In the 20th century, rivers were dammed to provide electricity.

The major deposits of iron ore are in Lapland, near the towns of Kiruna, Gällivare and Malmberget. Some of this ore is used to make iron and steel in Sweden, but most is exported. The iron ore is sent by rail to the Norwegian port of Narvik, because Swedish ports along the Gulf of Bothnia are frozen up in winter. Sweden also produces some gold, silver and copper, and exports refined zinc and lead.

KEY FACTS

● Of the total electricity supply, 52% is produced by hydro-electricity, 42% by nuclear power, and 6% from oil, coal and other sources.

● Nuclear power is a controversial issue. Parliament decided to close down 1 reactor in 1998. The remaining 11 reactors will probably be gradually shut down within the next 20 years.

● There are 60 major power stations in Sweden. Of these, 45 are hydro-electric stations and 4 are nuclear power generation plants with 2 to 4 reactors each.

● Cheap energy is an important resource for some sectors of the industry, especially for those factories producing pulp and paper.

Timber, pulp and paper make up 18% of the total exports. The most important timber-producing areas are in the southern half of the country, where trees grow faster than in the north.

Half the electricity that is consumed in Sweden comes from water power, and the rest mainly from nuclear reactors. As electricity is cheaper in Sweden than in most other countries, it is used to power industry and to heat the majority of houses. Oil, however, still has to be imported. Over the next few decades, nuclear power will be phased out, so Sweden is now looking for alternative energy sources. New ways of producing energy are being explored such as SUSTAINABLE FORESTS with fast growing trees that can be used in special furnaces for generating electricity and heating.

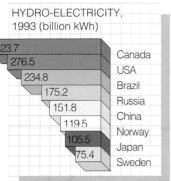

LEAD ORE PRODUCTION, 1993 (thousand tonnes)
Australia 544
354
Mexico
218
181
USA
Peru
111
182
Sweden
Canada

HYDRO-ELECTRICITY, 1993 (billion kWh)

323.7	Canada
276.5	USA
234.8	Brazil
175.2	Russia
151.8	China
119.5	Norway
105.5	Japan
75.4	Sweden

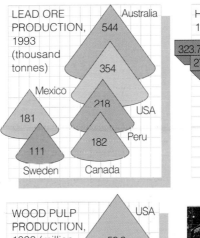

WOOD PULP PRODUCTION, 1993 (million tonnes)
USA 58.3
Japan
10.6
23.7
10.2
Canada
Sweden

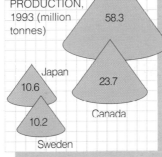

◄ *A saw mill. The sawdust is often used to make boards or pellets for boilers.*

▲ *Logging often takes place during the winter months. The frozen ground makes transport easier.*

⊞ POPULATION

Compared to most countries, Sweden is not densely populated with an average of approximately 20 inhabitants per square kilometre. The population density, however, differs widely from north to south. In Lapland, there is only about one person per square kilometre, but in the southern third of the country, where 80% of Swedes live, there are 48 people per square kilometre.

Population growth is slow, with a natural increase of only a few thousand each year, from 0.1 to 0.2%. Immigration has, however, meant that the population has increased at a higher rate than this in recent years.

From the end of the 19th century, people

◄ *Drottninggatan is a long pedestrianized street in central Stockholm, popular with shoppers.*

LIFE EXPECTANCY, 1995	
80	Japan
79	Sweden
79	Hong Kong
78	Switzerland
78	France
78	Norway
78	Netherlands
78	Canada
78	Italy
78	Greece
77	Belgium
77	UK
77	USA
77	Australia
77	Austria
77	Ireland

► *A residential area in Stockholm on the shore of Mälaren, one of the largest lakes in Sweden.*

began to move from rural areas into industrial towns and cities. Today 83% of Swedes live in urban areas. A third of them have settled in and around the three largest cities, Stockholm, Göteborg and Malmö.

The Government has set up programmes in the rural areas, the north and in the islands to create more jobs. These have not been very successful in persuading people to stay. Young people, especially, leave because of better opportunities in the cities.

The physical features of the Swedes do not differ much from the north to the south of the country. Although many are tall with fair hair, this is not always the case. There are many exceptions, as people have, for centuries, migrated to Sweden from neighbouring countries and the European continent.

There are some small, long-established minorities. The largest minority group consists of some 30,000 Finnish speaking

KEY FACTS

● Swedish is spoken in Finland by about 300,000 people or 6% of the population. The biggest concentration of Swedish speakers is on the island of Åland and its archipelago, where Swedish is the official language. This is a result of six centuries of Swedish rule over Finland.

● The Swedish alphabet has three letters, å, ä and ö, that do not exist in the English language. They come at the end of the Swedish alphabet, after z. The small dots and circles over the letters are important for correct pronunciation.

● Since 1954, a Nordic labour market has been established. This allows citizens of Denmark, Finland, Iceland, Norway and Sweden to live and work in any of these countries without a work permit.

● Since 1995, Sweden has been a member of the European Union (EU) which allows citizens of any of its 15 member countries to work and live anywhere inside the EU.

● In 1749, Sweden became the first country in the world to keep detailed population statistics. From this date onward, records exist giving the exact number of inhabitants in each town and village.

● Sweden's population growth: 0.9 million (1571); 1.4 million (1700); 2 million (1767); 3 million (1835); 4 million (1863); 5 million (1897); 6 million (1923); 7 million (1950); 8 million (1969); 8.9 million (1998).

inhabitants of the Torne river valley in the north. The Lapps, who number about 17,000, usually live in the mountains of northern Sweden. About 2,500 of them still make a living from reindeer herding. Others have moved to towns in search of jobs. There are also 20,000 Jews and 7,000 gypsies.

During the last few decades, the number of New Swedes (immigrants from other countries) has increased. Some of these New Swedes came in the period from about 1950 to 1980, looking for jobs. Most of them came from neighbouring countries, especially Finland. Later, refugees fled to Sweden from wars in the Middle East, Africa and the former Yugoslavia.

The arrival of large numbers of immigrants has caused some problems, especially in the suburbs of the big cities. Here, people who look or dress differently feel that they are discriminated against and

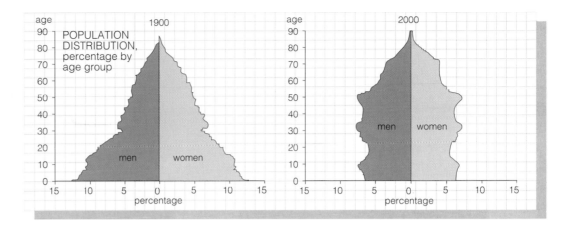

◄ *This photograph shows a ceremony welcoming immigrants to Hallunda, a suburb of Stockholm that has a large percentage of immigrants.*

exposed to racial prejudice.

Some of the more recent arrivals have not been integrated as well as the earlier immigrants were. They often live together in the suburbs of the big cities. In the Stockholm area, one in six inhabitants was born outside Sweden.

Today almost one in ten inhabitants of Sweden were born abroad. Many have become Swedish citizens. They can do this after they have lived in the country for five years. Others expect to return to their home countries, when peace has been restored there. Most immigrants learn Swedish; this is essential if they are to get a job. Even so, unemployment amongst immigrants is high.

Swedish is the mother tongue for native Swedes. There are many dialects but people can easily understand one another. Lapps have their own language, but most of them also speak Swedish. Finnish is still the mother tongue for most of the 200,000 people of Finnish origin living in Sweden.

As Sweden is a small country and Swedish is rarely spoken outside its borders, all Swedish students learn English as a foreign language, starting at the age of nine or ten. Many also learn French, German and other commonly spoken languages.

▼ *A Lapp in traditional costume with his prize-winning reindeer.*

LEISURE

Because of the climate, people's lifestyle changes considerably from summer to winter. During the long, warm summer days people spend a lot of time in the open air, but it is so cold and dark in winter that people tend to use their spare time differently. For young people to make the most of the summer, there is a ten-week school holiday from early June to late August, whereas the winter holidays are very short.

Most Swedes enjoy outdoor life. City people often have a summer house, where they spend holidays and weekends. Often these houses are well insulated, so that they can also be used during the winter as a starting point for skiing, or long-distance skating trips. Because of the long coast line and the many islands, most people own a boat so that they can go sailing.

Access to the countryside is guaranteed by tradition and law. It was once important

KEY FACTS

● Orienteering originated in Sweden. It combines skills in map reading and cross-country running. Today, it is becoming popular all over the world.

● Long-distance skating is very popular in those areas of Sweden where lakes, rivers and the water around the groups of islands freeze during winter.

● Many Swedes (40%) live in privately-owned villas and terraced houses, 15% in privately-owned apartments, and 45% in rented apartments and houses.

● In Sweden, 1 out of 3 people have access to the Internet, via their telephones and computers.

for the poor to be able to pick berries and mushrooms to supplement an otherwise poor diet. Today, everybody has access to privately-owned forests and most other areas for walking, for picking berries and for swimming. No one is allowed, however, to chop down trees or to go too close to inhabited houses. There are also laws restricting the exploitation of the seashore to keep it accessible to the public.

WORK

The working week is generally 35–40 hours long, but many people, especially women, only work part-time. Swedes have a minimum of five weeks paid holiday each year in addition to public holidays.

EDUCATION

As both parents often work, most children attend state or private nurseries from the age of about two. School is compulsory between the age of 7 and 16, but many children start their education at 6 and most of them continue until they are 19.

There are private schools, but generally Swedish children are educated at schools run by local authorities. For the first nine years, everybody follows more or less the same curriculum. During the final two years, students can make some individual choices, like taking an extra foreign language or studying a more advanced course of mathematics.

HOLIDAYS AND RELIGIOUS FESTIVALS	
January 1	NEW YEAR'S DAY
January 6	TWELFTH NIGHT (Epiphany)
March/April	EASTER
April 30	VALBORG, or WALPURGIS An ancient festival when bonfires are lit and students sing to greet the coming of spring.
May 1	LABOUR DAY
May	ASCENSION DAY
Early June	PENTECOST
Late June	MIDSUMMER People traditionally dance around the maypole.
Early November	ALL SAINTS' DAY
December 13	LUCIA DAY
December 24–26	CHRISTMAS

More than nine out of ten students continue for another three years of school from the age of 16 to 19, during which period they can choose between a number of options. Some study a programme of academic subjects in preparation for university. Others take a mixture of

◀ *People enjoying a coffee and a chat in the medieval Stortorget (Great Square) in the old town of Stockholm.*

▶ *There are many women police officers in Sweden. Here, one has stopped to pass the time of day with a senior citizen.*

◀ A popular winter sport is bandy, a Scandinavian form of ice hockey, played with curved sticks and a ball. The Swedish championship finals are one of the biggest sporting events of the year.

▶ Dog-sledge races are held on frozen lakes and are especially popular during the long winters of northern Sweden.

academic and vocational subjects in order to become skilled workers, like carpenters, car mechanics or hairdressers.

Discipline problems are increasing in Swedish schools. This is partly because classes have become larger due to budget cuts, and also because a larger proportion

of teenagers stay on at school today, including some who are poorly motivated.

Swedish classrooms are informal. Pupils always call their teachers by their first names. Since the 1960s, Swedes have stopped using formal methods of address in schools as well as in the workplace.

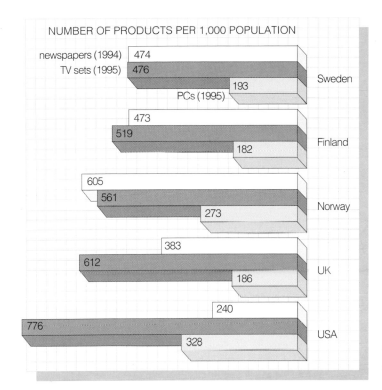

NUMBER OF PRODUCTS PER 1,000 POPULATION

newspapers (1994)
TV sets (1995)
PCs (1995)

Sweden
474
476
193

Finland
473
519
182

Norway
605
561
273

UK
383
612
186

USA
240
776
328

Sport plays an important part in daily life. Football and ice hockey are the most popular sports and are played by most Swedish children, girls as well as boys. Others prefer tennis, table tennis, swimming, horse riding, orienteering, skiing and skating. Adults often take up jogging, body building and golf to keep fit.

Evening classes are very popular for both young people and adults. These are encouraged by Government grants. People study such things as photography, art, chess or foreign languages. Originally, evening classes were introduced by the

▼ **The rock duo, Roxette, in Helsinki, one of many Swedish groups that have become popular abroad.**

labour movement and the teetotaller associations in the late 19th century to help the poor and uneducated improve themselves. Today, when people are better educated, the main purpose is to offer meaningful spare-time activities and to keep young people occupied.

Almost every home has a television set and most families have a computer. Many people spend several hours a day watching television and video films or surfing the Internet.

INFANT MORTALITY, 1980–95 (per 1,000)	1980		1995
Sweden	7		4
Japan	8		4
Norway	8		5
UK	12		6
USA	13		8
Sierra Leone	190		179
Cambodia	201		108
India	116		68
Sri Lanka	34		16

RELIGION

More than nine out of ten Swedes belong to a Christian church, but less than half practise their religion. The Lutheran Church, the state church of Sweden since the 16th century, is the largest of these.

Other Protestant Christian movements

are the Pentecostalists, Baptists, Methodists and the Salvation Army. There are also 150,000 Catholics in Sweden, while several thousand immigrants from Greece, the former Yugoslavia, the Middle East, Russia and Ukraine belong to Orthodox churches.

The largest non-Christian religion is Islam with some 130,000 followers, most of whom are immigrants from the Middle East. There are also about 20,000 Jews, 15,000 Buddhists and 5,000 Hindus.

◄ *Children of a fourth grade class performing an experiment during a science lesson at the Bombacka School, in Södertälje.*

▶ *In a ceremony held in Uppsala Cathedral in 1997, Christina Odelberg was consecrated as the first woman bishop of the Lutheran church in Sweden. In 1998, a second female bishop was appointed.*

RULE AND LAW

Prime Minister Göran Persson (top centre) with his cabinet at Harpsund, the official country retreat of the Swedish Government.

THE GOVERNMENT

RIKSDAGEN (Parliament)

Prime Minister

Speaker

About 20 ministers

349 members

In recent elections 6–7 parties have been represented in Parliament

'All public power comes from the people' (The Swedish Constitution)
All Swedish Citizens from the age of 18 have the right to vote in elections to Parliament and the provincial and local assemblies

Sweden is one of few remaining monarchies in Europe, but the king or queen has no political power, only a symbolic role. The Prime Minister and his ministers govern the country. Parliament has the power to make laws and decide on the budget, while the law courts are independent.

The Swedish Parliament, Riksdagen, first met in Arboga in 1435. It has gradually changed over the centuries to become more representative of the population as a whole.

Riksdagen has 349 members in a single chamber. Elections to the Parliament and to regional and local assemblies take place every four years and all Swedes have the right to vote from the age of 18.

Major political parties are the Social Democrats, the Moderates, the Left Party, People's Party, the Centre Party, the Christian Democrats and the Environmental Party.

KEY FACTS

● Women make up 40% of the Members of Parliament. This is a higher proportion than any other country in the world.
● The election system is based on proportional representation, and each party presents the voters with a list of its candidates. A party with, for instance, 20% of the votes will have 20% of the seats in the Parliament. However, for a party to get members elected, it must get a minimum of 4% of the total vote.
● Participation in elections is usually high. Generally 80 to 90% of those eligible to vote will go to the polls.
● Sweden is a hereditary monarchy and the crown is passed to the eldest child. The present king, Carl Gustav XVI, will be succeeded by his daughter, Crown Princess Victoria.

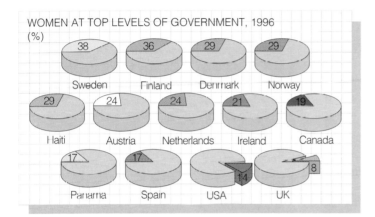

WOMEN AT TOP LEVELS OF GOVERNMENT, 1996 (%)

Sweden 38
Finland 36
Denmark 29
Norway 29
Haiti 29
Austria 24
Netherlands 24
Ireland 21
Canada 19
Panama 17
Spain 17
USA 14
UK 8

◄ *Anna Maltinger, a 22-year-old Swedish airforce pilot, one of a small but increasing number of women in the Swedish armed forces.*

communications, and they also run community services.

In 1809, the Swedish Parliament introduced the post of Ombudsman. This is a Swedish word meaning 'representative'. The independence of this post is guaranteed by law and the constitution. The Ombudsman's role is to hear complaints from the public and put a stop to corruption and the abuse of power by the central and local governments. This Swedish institution, and the word 'Ombudsman' has been adopted by many other countries. There are now several similar institutions in Sweden to which people can complain if they feel they have been unfairly treated by the media or discriminated against because of their sex or race.

The country was, until recently, divided into 24 provinces, but a process is now under way to reorganize the provincial administration into larger units. There are 289 local communities of varying size, each of which have their local assembly. Provincial and local bodies decide on issues like hospitals, schools and local

► *King Carl Gustav shaking hands with President Nelson Mandela during a visit to South Africa, with former President F. W. de Klerk waiting his turn.*

FOOD AND FARMING

▲ *A family enjoying an outdoor meal during Midsummer celebrations on the island of Bergöklubben, in the Baltic Sea.*

Food production in Sweden has undergone dramatic changes during the 20th century. This is particularly true of the period after the Second World War, when agriculture became more mechanized. In 1950, 25% of the Swedish work force was employed in agriculture. Now it is only about 2.5%.

The land area used for farming has decreased from about 3.5 million hectares in 1950 to 2.8 million today. In the same period, the number of farms has dropped from about 270,000 to about 90,000. Many small farms have been sold to owners of larger units while, in other cases, farm land

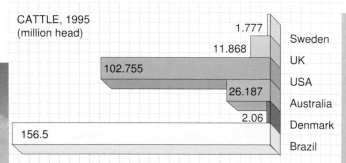

CATTLE, 1995 (million head)

Sweden	1.777
UK	11.868
USA	102.755
Australia	26.187
Denmark	2.06
Brazil	156.5

has been converted into forests or used for producing fast-growing trees for energy production.

Even so, food imports have shrunk from about 20% of total imports in the 1950s to 8% in the 1990s. The main reason for this is that productivity has been increased by mechanization and improved farming techniques. A more controversial cause is the increased use of ARTIFICIAL FERTILIZERS, PESTICIDES and HERBICIDES.

Animal farming has changed more than any other sector of agriculture. As in many European countries, meat, milk, poultry and eggs are produced by intensive, factory-farming methods. Most animals are

▲ *Agricultural land on the shore of Lake Vättern, in the county of Småland, southern Sweden.*

◀ *Dairy cattle on a traditional farm, near Uppsala, central Sweden.*

KEY FACTS

● Production of meat, milk, dairy products and eggs make up about two-thirds of the income of Swedish farmers.

● A typical Swedish farm is small with less than 20 hectares of land. It gives employment to only 1 person. Only about 10,000 farms are big enough to give full-time employment to 2 or more people.

● Food processing employs about 75,000 people. Most of it takes place in big units owned by the farmers, who have organized themselves in big CO-OPERATIVES for this purpose.

● Some farms near urban areas grow strawberries and blackcurrants where people come to pick the fruit themselves. Other farmers welcome visitors and take in paying guests during the summer months. Farm visits are becoming very popular and give young people a chance to see what life is like in the country.

kept indoors. Cows are fed artificial feed and milked mechanically, while many chickens and pigs are kept in battery cages and pens.

These production methods and the intensive use of chemicals have been condemned by many consumers. Because of this, there is a move towards more environmentally friendly practices and a return to traditional farming methods. Farmers are increasingly letting their cows into meadows to graze and some farms are producing eggs from free-range hens. Other organic farms specialize in growing cereals and vegetables without the use of any chemicals.

Some land, especially on the island of Gotland and in northern Sweden, which was once used for growing crops, has been converted into pasture for sheep. Reindeer herding for meat and skins is still important to the economy of some 2,500 Lapp people, in 51 villages in the northern part of

Sweden. Animals either graze in the lowland forest areas or are moved between mountain slopes in summer and forest areas in winter, in search of good pastures. Today, herdsmen use snow scooters and helicopters to drive their animals whereas, traditionally, Lapps travelled on skis.

The most important agricultural areas are located in the plains of southern Sweden, where more than half of all farmland is to be found. Wheat and oil seeds are the main crops in this region. There are also areas in the south specializing in the production of fruit and vegetables. Further north, where the climate is less favourable, crops for fodder and potatoes are more important.

Often people who own small farms have other jobs beside agriculture. Especially in the north, and in the southern highlands, forestry is a common secondary occupation. Others have taken up part-time work in neighbouring towns.

◀ *A coastal village where fish are hanging out to dry. This is a traditional way of preserving the catch, far removed from the big plants of the modern fishing industry.*

Although Swedish food production has become very efficient in the post-war era, production costs are expensive. Because of this, any surplus products are difficult to sell on the international market, as prices are high. Parliament has, therefore, decided to give incentives to farmers who decide to reduce their cereal and milk production.

Not everyone agrees with this policy, as it is likely to result in a further movement from villages to towns.

Fishing is mainly carried out from ports along the west coast and in the Baltic Sea.

▼ *A fruit and vegetable market in Malmö, the largest city in the major agricultural area of Skåne, in southern Sweden.*

Herring is the most important catch. The number of full-time fishermen has dropped from about 20,000 in 1950 to some 4,000 today. Fishing accounts for only about 0.1% of Sweden's GROSS DOMESTIC PRODUCT (GDP) but is important to people in coastal villages and to those living along the shores of the larger lakes.

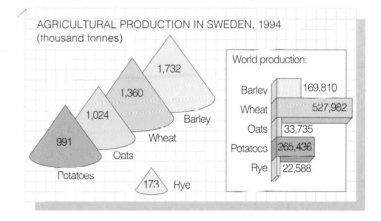

AGRICULTURAL PRODUCTION IN SWEDEN, 1994 (thousand tonnes)

- 1,732 Barley
- 1,360 Wheat
- 1,024 Oats
- 991 Potatoes
- 173 Rye

World production:
- Barley 169,810
- Wheat 527,982
- Oats 33,735
- Potatoes 265,436
- Rye 22,588

✚ TRADE AND INDUSTRY

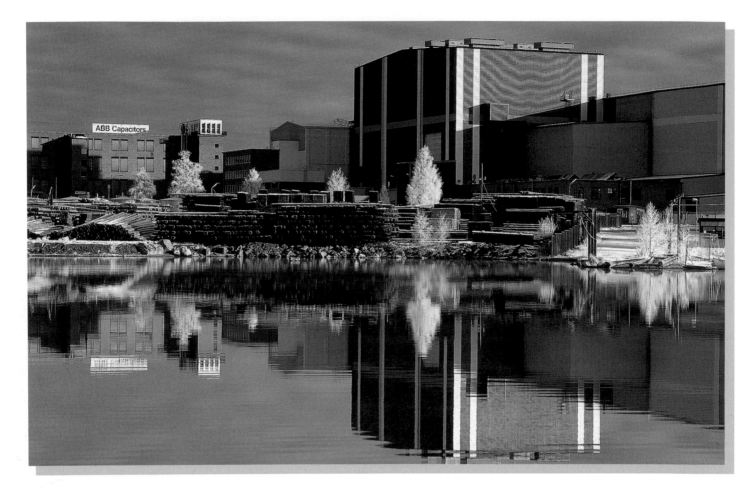

Sweden is a highly industrialized country and the export of manufactured products is extremely important for its economy. Even so, more people are employed in trade and services than in factories. Because the production processes in so many factories have become AUTOMATED, the number of industrial employees has dropped sharply during the last few decades. Only one Swede out of five is employed by an industrial company compared to almost one in two around 1950.

This is because Sweden, where labour is expensive, has been facing increasing competition from countries where labour is cheap. This has led to the increasing use of sophisticated machinery in Swedish factories. Today, computers and industrial

▲ **With an industrial tradition going back to the 16th century, the town of Ludvika is still an important centre for manufacturing. Asea Brown Bovery (ABB), which makes generators and industrial robots, is the major employer.**

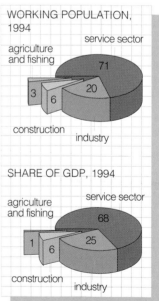

WORKING POPULATION, 1994

agriculture and fishing

service sector

71

3 6 20

construction

industry

SHARE OF GDP, 1994

agriculture and fishing

service sector

68

1 6 25

construction

industry

robots have taken over many jobs that previously were done manually. The high cost of labour has even made some large companies, such as Volvo and Ericsson, transfer the manufacture of some parts of their cars and telephones to other countries.

Industries that require a lot of manual labour, like the manufacture of clothing, are now becoming less important. Factories have shifted from making simple products to manufacturing more complex products like sophisticated machinery, and electrical and electronic equipment. Highly qualified and highly skilled employees are needed to manufacture these goods. Telecommunication systems and mobile telephones, cars and heavy vehicles, power generators and industrial robots are just some of the major products of Swedish engineering companies.

Other important industrial products are

KEY FACTS

● More than 500,000 people are employed in Swedish-owned companies outside Sweden, while 200,000 people are employed in Sweden by foreign-owned companies.

● Sweden's most important trading partners are Germany, the UK, the USA and Japan.

● A high proportion of Swedish industrial workers are employed in large factories. Some 35% work for companies with more than 500 employees and only 6% in units with 20 people or less.

● Foreign investors own about a quarter of the value of shares registered on the Stockholm stock exchange.

● It is vital for Sweden, like most other small countries, to be able to sell large quantities of goods abroad. This is why Sweden is a strong supporter of free trade.

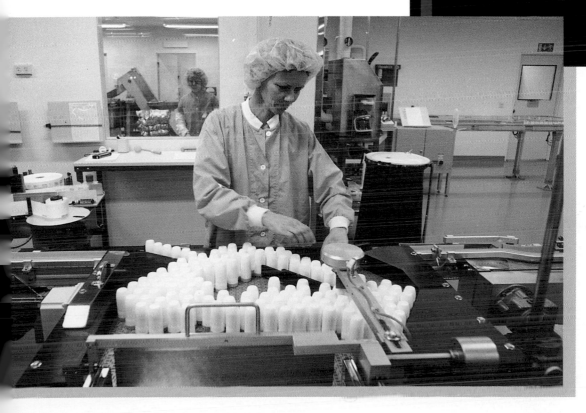

◀ *Inhalers for asthmatic patients are one of a wide range of products from the leading medical company Astra, with its main production units at Södertälje, south of Stockholm.*

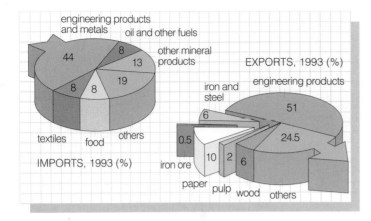

engineering products and metals 44
oil and other fuels 8
other mineral products 13
19
8
8
8
textiles
food
others

IMPORTS, 1993 (%)

EXPORTS, 1993 (%)

iron and steel 6
engineering products 51
24.5
iron ore 0.5
paper 10
pulp 2
wood 6
others

medicines, ball bearings and high-quality steel. Paper, produced in modern automated mills, has, to a large extent, replaced the export of pulp. Sweden also has its own defence industry, producing fighter bombers, submarines and guns for its own military forces as well as for export. But the export of arms is a controversial issue. Many people feel that it goes against the importance the Swedish Government and people place on promoting international peace.

Despite recent economic problems, Sweden is still an important industrial country. One reason for the success of its products is a tradition of industrial innovation. Alfred Nobel, who made a fortune from inventing dynamite, is probably the best known Swede. This is because of the world-famous Nobel prize that is financed by money from his business activities. In recent years,

◄ *A woman worker on the production line of Saab Automobile. This company is the second largest Swedish car manufacturer after Volvo.*

▲ *The Swedish airforce's most modern plane is the Saab Gripen. It has been offered for sale to several other countries.*

furniture from Ikea, clothes from Hennes & Mauritz and packaging from Tetra Pak are examples of Swedish products which started on a small scale with a simple idea and grew to become internationally well known.

Today most Swedes are employed in the service sector, in hospitals, schools, shops, banks and the transport industry. Service industries have expanded rapidly since the 1950s. Together with public administration, they employ about 3 million people, compared to 800,000 in industry.

In the late 1990s, the number of people working in the PUBLIC SERVICE SECTOR has been reduced because of lack of money. Some activities in the areas of health and

transport have been taken away from local government and given to private companies to run.

The fact that the number of people employed in industry and the public service sector has dropped, is one reason why unemployment is rising. More than 10% of the work force was out of work in the late 1990s. About half of those laid off were invited to join Government training programmes, aimed at training them in the skills they need to work in modern industry.

The Government has tried other ways of reducing unemployment. More young people are being encouraged to go on to university and early retirement is being offered to older employees. Trade unions have demanded shorter working hours and they have, in some cases, managed to negotiate small reductions. Companies have asked for tax reductions as a way to increase employment.

⊞ TRANSPORT

Sweden has a well developed transport system. This is important in a country where urban centres are considerable distances apart. With high speed trains, improved air transport and the construction of better roads, travelling time has been dramatically cut for today's travellers, and industrial products can now be moved more swiftly. This benefits large companies, such as car manufacturers, that make components in one place and assemble them in another.

In the 1990s, a number of fast trains, the X-2000s, were built for use between major cities. They run at a speed of 200 kilometres per hour. This is slower than the super-fast Japanese and French trains, but these Swedish-made trains can use existing tracks. This makes construction

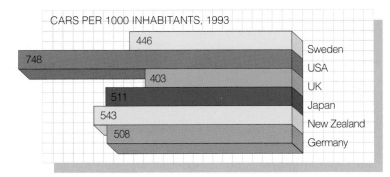

CARS PER 1000 INHABITANTS, 1993

446	Sweden
748	USA
403	UK
511	Japan
543	New Zealand
508	Germany

▼ **High speed trains, the X-2000s, now connect major cities, cutting the former travelling time in half.**

▲ **At Slussen, in Stockholm, there are connections between all forms of transport: trains, cars, buses, subway trains and ferries.**

cheaper. The train itself, and not the track, tilts when it runs through a bend.

After a period of decline, the railway system is being extended. This will make travel easier for people in the cities of the industrial belt west of Stockholm and in the northern coastal areas.

Air transport is still, however, the easiest way to travel around Sweden. A journey from Stockholm to Kiruna that will take 18–20 hours by train can be done by

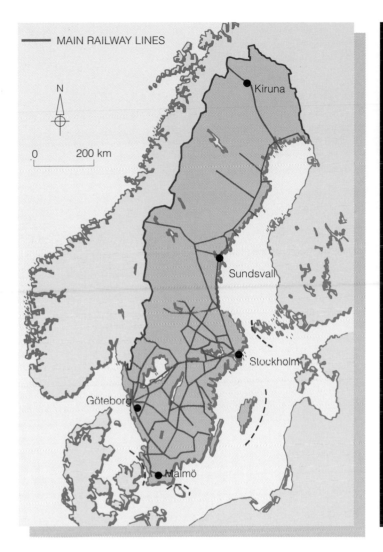

MAIN RAILWAY LINES

N

0   200 km

Kiruna

Sundsvall

Stockholm

Göteborg

Malmö

plane in about three hours, including travel to and from the airports.

The train and road systems are linked to the outside world by ferries carrying cars, trucks and, in many cases, railway wagons to Finland, Denmark, Germany, England and other countries. Smaller ferries take passengers and cars to Gotland and to the other islands. Some ports are kept open in winter by ice breakers which help shipping in the northern part of the Baltic Sea.

Snow and ice can make winter transport difficult, as severe blizzards occasionally block the roads and stop the rail traffic. With the help of big snow ploughs, traffic is kept going in all but the worst conditions.

▼ *A Stockholm underground station. The surface of the rock has been left in its natural state by the architect.*

37

▣ THE ENVIRONMENT

In Sweden, as in most industrial countries, the environment has suffered as a result of rapidly growing industries and towns. Land was cleared to make room for towns to expand, and for new factories and shopping centres to be built. Between the 1850s and 1950s, factories were constructed, rivers dammed and roads built. Little thought was given to the damage that was being done to the environment.

Only during the last quarter of a century, have the Swedes made a serious effort to protect the environment, and to stop the discharge of hazardous waste from industries, agriculture and road traffic. Even so it is likely to be difficult and costly to put right some of the damage already done.

Fortunately, there is still plenty of unspoilt countryside left in Sweden. Because of this, the environmental damage might not be as visible as it is in many other countries. However, dams have been built on most of the larger rivers to produce hydro-electricity. There has been irreparable damage done to sensitive forests in some mountain areas. Motorways now cut through the once unspoiled landscape, and towns are spreading into land that used to be fertile agricultural fields.

In the big cities, the worst problem is air pollution caused by cars and by boilers used for central heating. In spite of stricter controls over the type of fuel that is used, there has been little improvement as the number of cars has continued to increase.

Industrial discharge from factories has dropped considerably in recent years. New laws have made factories treat waste water before it is discharged into rivers, lakes or into the public drainage system. The public sewage system has also been dramatically improved. Many polluted lakes have now been cleaned up as a result of these measures.

Swedish farmers use far less chemicals than their counterparts in some other European countries. Even so, harmful

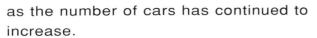 *A wolverine, one of many protected wild animals, that lives in the north of Sweden. As it kills reindeer, there is a conflict of interest between the reindeer-herding Lapps and animal conservationists.*

▶ *A swimmer diving into lake Mälaren from the stairs of the City Hall in Stockholm. Water quality has improved immensely since a modern sewage system has been installed in all the suburbs and other cities around the lake.*

substances from agriculture have had an effect on the countryside. Traces of pesticides have been found to be fatal to fish and other creatures. Fertilizers leak into lakes, rivers and the sea, encouraging the growth of algae, which uses up the oxygen in water. Because of this, there are less fish in the Baltic Sea and along the west coast than there use to be.

The environmental problems in the Baltic Sea are, to a large extent, caused by other countries, especially by waste from Russia, the Baltic states and Poland. Before the break up of the Soviet Union, the Communist Government paid little or no attention to environmental issues. Today, Swedish and other Scandinavian experts are working with officials in these countries to try to reduce industrial pollution and clean up the environment. The main reason for this is that any help given now should benefit Sweden itself in the future.

The unsafe condition of the nuclear power stations in the former Soviet Union is of particular concern to Sweden. Since the nuclear catastrophe in Chernobyl in 1986, which affected parts of Sweden badly, Swedish experts have been helping local engineers to improve the safety in these installations.

The use of nuclear power has been a major issue in Sweden, ever since the first commercial reactor was started up in 1972.

KEY FACTS

- There are 24 national parks and about 1,400 nature reserves in Sweden. The largest parks are located in the north. One of these covers as much as 5,000 square kilometres. The parks and reserves make up 6% of the total land area.
- In Sweden, 4% of all industrial investment is spent on measures aimed at improving the environment.
- 50% of paper and 59% of glass is recycled in Sweden.
- Swedish carbon dioxide emissions stand at 6.6 metric tonnes per capita (per head). This is about a third of that of the USA (19.1) but well above the world average of 4.0. In the UK, it is 9.8; in India, 0.9; in China, 2.3 and in the United Arab Emirates, 33.9.

GREENHOUSE GAS EMISSIONS, 1993
(thousand tonnes)

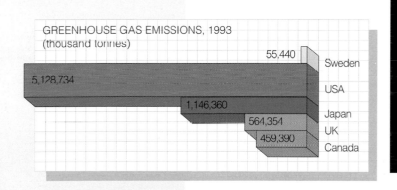

	thousand tonnes
Sweden	55,440
USA	5,128,734
Japan	1,146,360
UK	564,354
Canada	459,390

◄ Environment-alists protesting against the use of poisonous chemical materials during the digging of a tunnel for a new railway line. This will cut through a mountain at Båstad, southern Sweden.

The subject has been widely debated. In a referendum held in 1980, the voters gave a guarded yes to the use of this source of energy in the short term. On this basis, Parliament decided to allow twelve reactors to remain until the year 2010. Later, it was decided that one of these reactors would be shut down in 1998. No date has, as yet, been set for the shut down of the others. Those who think that this should be done as soon as possible, claim that energy is now being wasted because it is cheap. Others, who want the reactors to remain in use, say that the alternative to nuclear power is energy from coal and oil. They argue that these are even more harmful to nature than nuclear power.

⊟ THE FUTURE

For centuries, Sweden was a relatively isolated country. In the 20th century, with the development of modern systems of communication, Sweden has drawn closer to the rest of the world. At the same time, fast trains, telephone links, and computers connected to the Internet, have made communication within the country easier. Communications between the north and south of the country used to be difficult and slow. Now they are almost as easy as those between east and west.

Politically, Sweden moved closer to Europe when it became a member of the EU in 1995. Since the collapse of communism in the Soviet Union and Poland, it has become very important for Sweden that the Baltic Sea area remains

KEY FACTS

● By the year 2010, 1 out of 4 Swedes will be above the retiring age of 65. A huge fund has been created to safeguard the pension system.

● New sources of energy will have to be found by the year 2010 to replace Sweden's outdated nuclear reactors.

● Sweden is one of the 13 member countries of the European Space Agency (ESA). One of the ESA's projects is the European Space Programme. This has a ground station, named Esrange, near the town of Kiruna, north of the Arctic Circle. From there, space rockets are launched to study the atmosphere, including a phenomenon called the NORTHERN LIGHTS. It is part of a programme of peaceful space research started in 1975.

as stable as possible. The Government is working closely with neighbouring countries to secure peace in this area, to speed up economic development in the former Soviet republics, and to improve the environment. Because of pressure from Sweden, a council of co-operation, with all the Baltic Sea states as its members, has been set up.

For decades, Swedes have enjoyed a high standard of living. More recently they have also become used to the sophisticated technology that has moved into many homes.

However, there have also been some problems. The welfare state, which has developed since the 1930s, is in trouble.

A scientist studies data on the Northern Lights, an atmospheric phenomenon normally only seen in latitudes close to the Arctic Circle. During periods of magnetic storms, this beautiful sight can be seen in central and even southern Sweden. It is important for scientists to understand how it works, as it can disturb radio communications.

A rocket is launched at the space centre, Esrange, near Kiruna.

With an unemployment rate of around 10%, and an increasing number of pensioners, the burden of taxation has become too great for those who are in work. Because of this, Parliament has decided to cut some of the social benefits that Swedes have become accustomed to.

At the same time Sweden looks to the future. Because it is a small country, Sweden tries to promote international co-operation in the field of science. The Government also places great emphasis on research and innovation, so that the country will be able keep pace with other well-developed industrial countries in the future.

FURTHER INFORMATION

● SWEDISH EMBASSY
11 Montagu Place, London W1H 2AL
Provides general information on Sweden.

● SWEDISH TRADE COUNCIL
73 Welbeck Street, London W1M 8AN
Provides general information on Sweden.

● SVENSKA INSTITUTET
(SWEDISH INSTITUTE)
Sverigehuset, Box 7434,
S-103 91 Stockholm, Sweden
A Government agency offering information in the form of books and a number of fact sheets on such aspects as the culture,
political system, economy and environment of Sweden.

● SWEDISH TRAVEL
& TOURISM COUNCIL
11 Montagu Place, London W1H 2AL
Provides general information for visitors to Sweden.

BOOKS ABOUT SWEDEN
The National Atlas of Sweden, Volumes 1–17, SNA Publishing 1992 (age 14+)
The Modern Industrial World: Sweden;
Bo Kage Carlson, Wayland 1995 (age 12+)

GLOSSARY

ARTIFICIAL FERTILIZERS
Chemicals that are added to soil to help crops to grow.

AUTOMATED
When machinery is operated by computer-controlled processes or robots rather than by manual labour.

CO-OPERATIVE
A group of people who work together, rather than as individuals, sharing the costs of production and the profits.

GROSS DOMESTIC PRODUCT (GDP)
The total value of all the goods and services produced by a country in a year.

HERBICIDES
Chemicals that are used by farmers to kill weeds growing amongst crops.

ICE AGE
A period of time when ice sheets and glaciers advanced from the polar regions to cover areas that had previously had a
warmer climate. The last Ice Age ended in about 8,000 BC, when the ice finally retreated to its present position.

NORTHERN LIGHTS
This is an atmospheric phenomenon (sometimes known as the aurora borealis). It occurs when electrons that are rich in energy from the sun hit oxygen and nitrogen atoms in the upper atmosphere.

PESTICIDES
Chemicals that kill insects harmful to farmers' crops.

PUBLIC SERVICE SECTOR
Elements of the service sector, such as hospitals and social services, that are financed by a Government. These may vary from country to country.

SUSTAINABLE FORESTS
Forests where fast-growing trees are continuously being replanted to replace those that have been harvested.

INDEX